HENRY AND THERESA'S RACE

by Ronne Peltzman
illustrated by John Nez

Story based on the Aesop's Fable *"The Hare and the Tortoise"*

A GOLDEN BOOK • NEW YORK
Western Publishing Company, Inc., Racine, Wisconsin 53404

Copyright© 1984 by Western Publishing Company, Inc. Illustrations copyright© 1984 by John Nez. All rights reserved. Printed in the U.S.A. No part of this book may be reproduced or copied in any form without written permission from the publisher. GOLDEN®, GOLDEN & DESIGN®, A LITTLE GOLDEN BOOK®, and A GOLDEN BOOK® are trademarks of Western Publishing Company, Inc. Library of Congress Catalog Card Number: 83-83275 ISBN 0-307-10129-0 ISBN 0-307-68153-X (lib. bdg.) DEFGHIJ

Henry Hare lived in a burrow in the woods.
Theresa Tortoise lived by a stream near Henry's burrow.

Every day Henry visited Theresa.
He liked to talk to her.

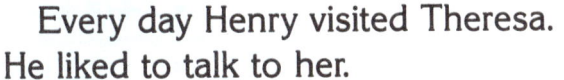

"I got five turnips from Mrs. Gilligan's garden," Henry said one day. "I am the cleverest animal in these woods."

"That's nice," said Theresa.

Another day, Henry saw his reflection in the stream.
"My, how long my ears are," he said. "I am the handsomest animal in these woods."
"That's nice," said Theresa.

One day Henry said, "Mrs. Gilligan tried to catch me this morning, but I ran away. I am the fastest animal in these woods."

But Theresa did not say, "That's nice."
She was tired of Henry's boasting.
"You may be fast," she said, "but I
can beat you in a race."

Henry laughed. "I have long, springy legs," he said. "You have short, stubby legs. I run fast. You walk slowly. I can win any race with you."

"All right," said Theresa. "Tomorrow we will race from here to Mrs. Gilligan's garden. We will see who gets there first."

The next day all the animals in the forest came out to watch the race. Everyone thought Henry would win. Only old Samuel Owl thought differently. "Fast is not always best," he said.

"Go!" shouted the animals, and the race began.

Henry ran fast on his long, springy legs. Theresa walked slowly on her short, stubby legs.

All the animals cheered. "Faster, Theresa, faster!" they called. But soon Henry was out of sight.

Henry ran through the woods and into the clearing.

He ran down the road and past the apple orchard.

"I am almost there," he said to himself. "Theresa will not catch up for hours. I can take a rest!"

He stretched out behind a hedge and fell fast asleep.

Meanwhile, Theresa kept walking. She walked slowly through the woods and into the clearing.

She walked slowly down the road and past the apple orchard.

She walked slowly past the hedge and right up to Mrs. Gilligan's garden.

Henry was not there. He was still fast asleep.

"Hooray for Theresa!" the animals shouted. "Theresa won the race!"

The noise woke Henry up. He ran to the garden.

"What's going on?" he asked when he saw everyone there.

"Theresa won," the animals said. "Theresa got here first."

"How can that be?" asked Henry. "I run so fast, and Theresa walks so slowly."

"You may run fast," said Theresa, "but you stopped before you were finished. I may walk slowly, but I did not stop until I got here."

"You see," said Old Samuel Owl, "fast is not always best. Sometimes slow and steady wins the race."